Pythagoras in Love

ALSO BY LEE SLONIMSKY

Talk Between Leaf and Skin

PYTHAGORAS

IN

LOVE

LEE SLONIMSKY

ORCHISES
WASHINGTON
2007

Library of Congress Cataloging in Publication Data

Slonimsky, Lee.
Pythagoras in love / Lee Slonimsky.
p. cm.
ISBN-13: 978-1-932535-13-6 (alk. paper)
I. Title

PS3619.L67P98 2007
811'.54—dc22

20066048343

ACKNOWLEDGEMENTS

I owe a great debt to my friend and mentor, Dr. Daniel Hoffman, who first introduced me to sonnet writing in his poetry workshop at the University of Pennsylvania, and whose support for my work has led to the publication of this book. The counsel and encouragement of several other poets, including Dr. Alfred Dorn, Rhina Espaillat, Margaret Holley, X. J. Kennedy, the late William Matthews, Richard Moore, Eric Ormsby, and Kevin Pilkington, has been crucial. I am thankful to my publisher, Roger Lathbury, for taking on this project and for his astute reading of an early draft, and to my wife Carol, daughter Nora, and my mother for their insightful feedback on individual poems.

Grateful acknowledgement is made to the editors of the following journals in which some of these poems first appeared, sometimes under different titles or in different form: *Best of Asheville Poetry Review, Blue Unicorn, Blueline, The Cape Rock, The Carolina Quarterly, The Classical Outlook, Connecticut Review, Connecticut River Review, Contemporary Rhyme, Green Hills Literary Lantern, Iambs & Trochees, The Lyric, The New York Times, Pivot, The Raintown Review, Sulphur River Literary Review,* and *Valparaiso Poetry Review.*

The first drafts of most of these poems were written on folded papers while I walked through two parks in northern New York City, Van Cortland and Inwood. Without the influence of their woods, hills, ponds, grassy fields and winding paths I might never have written a word.

Orchises Press
P. O. Box 20602
Alexandria, Virginia, 22320-1602

G6E4C2A

for Carol, Beloved

TABLE OF CONTENTS

1. THE LAST DIGIT OF PI

2. MONTHS THAT PROMISE YEARS

3. TEACHER IN THE WOODS

4. THE LONELINESS OF EXILE

5. MARRIAGE VOWS

1.

THE LAST DIGIT OF PI

THE LAST DIGIT OF PI

Bisected by a tree, the sun's gold light
draws angles on the glass skin of the pond;
dawn's revellers, a pair of geese in flight
soar high above the wooded hill, beyond
Pythagoras's line of sight. And now
he's all alone, high priest of water, sky,
intuiter of theorems, teller how
this world's the weave of math, the art of Pi.
Another pair of geese approach and glide
across the water, near the grove of trees
he sits beneath. Bird shadows try to hide
amidst the ripples wrinkled by a breeze.
The last of Pi's that stealthy, he decides,
elusive as the wind this dawn light rides.

WATCHING, DAY AND NIGHT

He sees the way a pair of gulls ascends,
as if their destination were the sun;
and wonders what the number two portends,
and if it's twice, or vastly more, than one.

Much later he spies geese that move as three,
their feathered arrow floating toward the west,
and wonders what significance could be
in triangles, as night delivers rest.

Four willows weep along the old stone fence
on which he sits, the sky pure darkness now;
he longs to make a perfect, mystic sense
of all the numbers earth and mind allow.

Perhaps dividing thirteen into seven
lies just beyond the starsplit door to heaven.

THE WORDS OF BIRDS

The triangle that dominates his dreams
will not reveal its hidden formula;
some nights, when its perfection truly gleams,
he whispers to the cosmos, "how you are

forever teasing me with truths of math,
elusive as my shadow as I go
along the spiral turns of my mind's path,
pursuing certainties no one can know."

He dreams for months before the truth arrives.
Awake, midday, he hears it in the way
a crow cries "caw" in threes, then fours, then fives—
not long now till he squares and then can say—

"I thank the cosmos for the counting birds
whose numbers are for them just like our words."

THREE-FOUR-FIVE

She caws in threes and fours as darkness falls.
Pythagoras observes this steadfast math
and wonders for how long the pattern lasts,
and when will she cry five, complete her call
so as to form a triangle of caws,
geometry of sound that can surpass
the numbered formulae that fill his past,
a black winged calculus that will spark awe.

But then, without a sign, the crow departs;
this randomness of fate gives him a chill.
He sees the beauty of wings merged with night,
but much prefers a math divinely willed
to rule this complex world and lovers' hearts
to perfect image of the crow's dark flight.

THE SWAN

Observing how the swan's two feet are webbed,
he wonders what role math played in design,
what abstract shapes were sewn, with flesh as thread,
into the swan's creation, lost in time.

The power of her wings as she takes flight
in clumsy but majestic dominance,
inspires him to count the beats of white
great feathered limbs against blue radiance.

As if such basic numbers could explain
the wizardry of feathers climbing air,
or give the essence of her flight a name,
describe perfection of her glide and soar.

If numbers could transform flesh readily,
he has no doubt what creature he would be.

AWAITING HIS TUTOR

First slant of warm May light bisects the sky,
in equal angles formed of scarlet glaze;
if only he could calculate a Pi
that, multiplied by dawn, predicts the breeze
caressing olive leaves that dangle near
his window struck by arrowing red rays,
his tutor would be thrilled. He cannot bear
to disappoint so early in the day.
But Pi exasperates the greatest minds
(except for one discovered long ago);
in feverish youth, he can't expect to find
prophetic numbers, calculus that shows
the math which summons morning breeze from light.

He hears his tutor's wings beating in flight.

TEACHER

His favorite pond suggests the rule of shapes,
this morning as a drizzle softly falls:

the triangles geese ripple in their wakes
while gliding near the rain glazed granite wall
on which he sits, and then the circles formed
each time a raindrop strikes the pond's clear skin.

The rain subsides, slow morning brightens, warms,
and now he's seen the way the world begins:
geometry, reflected in the pond,
as elemental as the summer air,
as perfect as the circling hawks beyond
the nearby hills, a math that's everywhere.

He leaves an offering before he goes.
The pond has been his teacher; now it knows.

AT THE POND

This goose's bobbing head, not far from shore,
is teaching water his geometry;
each undulating motion ripples more
and more round gleaming waves. Now he can see
how perfect circles are, beyond mere chance;

and geese as well are scholars, write the truth
with bobbing bills, intent as in a trance
that's conjured up by sunlight's gleam and math
upon this pond's noonbright quicksilver skin.
The water studies eagerly, the sun
contributes knowledge; now new theorems spin
and spark new ways of reasoning.
                                                            For one,
he contemplates how perfect nature's art;
how light and circles gave this world its start.

A CROW'S POINT OF VIEW

His morning walk reveals geometry
in how the sunlight angles through the trees
and intersects the mists that wreathe the pond;

a loud crow lectures oak leaves just beyond
his line of sight on how a dappled breeze
confuses light. And yes, he must agree
that shadows lie, that rippling branches tease
false theorems from the axes of sun's rays.

And yet, when air is still, the water gleams
with trapezoids and ellipses; sunbeams
seem shining summaries of all the ways
to measure surfaces. Dangling oak leaves

and pond instruct him well in ray-seamed math:
his new academy, a woodland path.

ANOTHER'S EYES

Pythagoras recalls how, as a tree,
he learned that math predicts both sun and shade,
perceived the numbers that the gods had made
to count the twigs and branches draped with leaves.
Such longing he felt then, to know how free
the birds were in their flight, light in the glade,
while stillness was the god that he obeyed,
and silent green of leaves his destiny.

He walks now, as a man, in just the woods
he lived in as an oak a hundred years,
no longer with that lust to move, speak, cry,
but thinking that he'd welcome, if he could,
another life now, as a fox or deer,
the revolution of another's eyes.

2.

MONTHS THAT PROMISE YEARS

PHILOSOPHER IN LOVE

The way her skin is bronzed by sunlit winds
that dapple cloud etched shadows across this hill,
suggests to him how fierily love begins,
reflecting a primordial heat, until,
its fuel consumed, it starts to chill and char,
till vanishing without one rosy trace.
Such brevity afflicts the largest star,
still mortal even as it brightens space,
and even stolid rock, that never breathes;

for him eternity's in numbers: One
the most perfect, like his great love, bequeathes
a universe benevolent and full
of radiance beyond the physical,
alongside eyes as bright as molten sun.

MONTHS THAT PROMISE YEARS

Perfection's meant the shape of spheres, the sun's
late day trajectory, an abacus
and how it measures rain, the scythesharp glide
of hawks, these swallows' swoops.
He's never dreamed...

of eyes more luminescent than star-fire,
of laughter lathering an ecstasy
as inexpressible as rosy dusk,
embraces hotter than noon's haze and yet
as bódiless as time, as fleeting winds,

that make a world as flawless as a line,
a circle, square, hypotenuse, designs
of falcons that know Pi,
infinity.

Love is perfection's deepest mystery,
Elena sunlight's slant on Harmony.

FAREWELL

The ship's dark shape drifts slowly toward the sun,
whose flaming sphere floats briefly on the sea;
Elena's face, which he'll no longer see
invades his thoughts: his suffering's begun.
Impossible, that she and he are done!
Yet as the ship turns dot there's no more "we,"
and once it vanishes their history
is boundaried in the past, like time undone,
as hard to cling to as the pink twilight,
or salt veined breezes winging past the shore.

The sun descends; eternal victor night
engulfs the presence that he so adores.
No theorem will console him; it's his fate
to understand his heart an hour too late.

RETURN TO THE SEAWALL

A flower stubbornly clings to a stone,
the tiniest of crevices its earth;
its white and purple petals find their berth
between two funnels of bright silver foam
a dozen feet above Poseidon's home,
where ceaseless tides rotate in bubbling mirth
and streaks of sorrow, blurs, like death and birth.
A spear of color, brief, and so alone...

its bloom will measure summer's lapse to fall,
and not another moment. Autumn comes
in dark gray clouds and frigid northern winds.
So desperate for distraction, he finds sums
and quotients to reveal how love begins.
But math is empty. Sad, he walks the wall.

VISIT TO A SEASIDE TEMPLE

This architecture is a symphony,
its stone columns a movement in the wind,
proportioned to an algebraic sea,
with granite waves that can't begin or end.

Its calculus evokes a tide of sound,
the way sun rays sing angles of desire;
its harmony reveres the square, and round,
and triangles which shape divine design.

Yet there's a void which troubles his rapt gaze,
an emptiness that gleaming rock can't fill,
that won't be soothed by stone's music until
Elena once again shares his gray days.

He listens to the waves' spray-shimmering hymns,
and prays their dazzling light brings her to him.

FLOWERS

It's early spring; the only flowers now
are blooming clouds reflected in the sea
wind-laced with light as far as he can see,
up to earth's end, where he would sail or row
if that would bring Elena back somehow.
But she's betrothed to foreign royalty,
forever lost to him in Sicily.
No theorem can outwit her marriage vow.

What soft and silver harbingers of spring,
these mirrored fluffs that grace the salty waves;
their lattice-work of rolling light near saves
him from the frosty wither absence brings.
Yet water-petals soon seem kin to lies,
as day tides on amidst gulls' hungry cries.

3.

TEACHER IN THE WOODS

TEACHER IN THE WOODS

The drifting light that settles in these leaves
creates a pathway of translucent green;
Pythagoras must pause, so he can glean
the meaning of this glow, what sun achieves
with startling luminescence for these trees
whose latticework of shine so brightly gleams
on up to verdant crowns, a green-gold seam
between dense hilly woods and soft spring breeze.

The sun is teaching math, this cool May day,
to every leaf and branch that understands
geometry, the gospel of its rays.
This is the only meaning he can find.
Each arrowed ray to earth's a perfect sign
for angle, number shown to trees and man.

REVELATION

The way sunlight is latticed by these leaves,
suggests a craftsmanship skilled and sublime,
some artisan of greenery and time;
geometry of light. The sun achieves,
in dappled shimmer, angles he perceives
as logic-luminescence, even mime
of his most crucial theorems. Paradigms.

Perhaps the sun is able to conceive
of numbers organizing earth and skies,
as shown when he counts rays that bloom on leaves,
dividing them to form a kind of prime
accounting for the beauty sunlight weaves.

And what a revelation, through his eyes:
to learn the formulae sunlight decrees.

THE LEGACY OF ORPHEUS

A secret language weaves its way through notes
of thrushes harmonizing in a glade,
so sun-ripe, violet flowered, slender leaved;

Pythagoras, concealed in deepest shade,
is listening for patterns from their throats
to illustrate what Orpheus believed:

no greater sage than woods, no man more wise;
and who more fit to speak for trees than birds,
their harmonies so apt they conjure words
from sunsoaked breeze to please his math-rapt ear?
No glossary required; truths arise
from every measured song diverting air:

thrush sequences are lush geometry
explaining light to wind in key of "C."

AUTHOR

So many languages, he hears at dawn:
the whispering of sunlight through these leaves,
translation of green tongues by a soft breeze,
the echoed verse of Orpheus in song
of thrush and mockingbird.
                                        He starts to tease
a language from how branches sway, birds glide
on rising sun's leaf latticed, wind kissed tide,
geometry from shadow, sun at play,
a theorem of benevolence from light.

Someday he'll try a whole translation of
the phrases that the sun's white letters write
as curlicued by greenery above;

his Chapter One this dawn in early May,
his theme how great the eloquence of light.

TEXT

These warblers lather air, soft rings of sound
that mirror ripples stonestruck on the pond,

green water's curved geometry of gleam,
light's shimmer-imitation of a text

(note soaked and legible as scribbled clouds)

he reads from memory on his slow walk:

papyrus weightless
                    as a breeze that streams
beneath a gliding hawk's unerring wings
and splashes sunlight,
                    blankly quickening
straight rays to ripples. He has memorized
the way waves splinter over rocks. Green shards

of glimmer are the footnotes to oblongs,
ellipses, circles, all the other forms
that flirt with chaos, marry formulae.

MOMENT OF DOUBT

The slender willows swaying in this pond—
reflections, yet as real as noon sunlight,
as wind caressing all the trees beyond
the rocky shore—
                                        are soothing to the sight,
but threaten theorems of pure harmony
by questioning what's vision and what's real,
dividing senses from reality;
the truth's a prize that shimmer's wiles conceal.

He shudders now in contemplation how
he can't rely on math, geometry;
all thinking's faith, mere matter space, and so
true essence more than he will ever see;

yet solace too, these willows kissed by light,
this tale of love that sky and water write.

LECTURER IN THE MIRROR

This sorcery by mirror of clear lake
in how it conjures up a gliding hawk,
ghostly companion to her mate above,
absorbs Pythagoras. His morning walk
becomes a tour of wizardry; the fake
blue water sky is shimmering with love
of early light for cloud and pond; sun-math
of sharp ray-angles striking water's glass
is lectured on in syllables of flight
that sums up clouds, triangulates the light
born in the east. Suggesting, now, a path
of glimmer through a chiseled world of facts,
illumining thought's soar. Mirrors may lie,
but do it perfectly, as pond gleams sky.

ATTENDING A LECTURE

The way the water polishes these stones
to text of perfect gleam, reminds him of
brisk wind's effect on light. Now, just above
a hawk revises ellipses to curves,
more basic shapes, a first geometry
the world knew before birth. Such nuanced swerves
that waltz with rays, more deft than any math,
suggest a genius even atoms have,
and he's been lacking lately. Sharp despair
at six months without theorems glooms his bones
and slows his blood, along a dappled path
where latticed sun-patterns once made forms clear.
But then a rhombus of clear rippling gleam,
wingsplit, inspires. New theorem's in this stream.

THE STUDY OF FLIGHT

Intelligence beyond his puny math:

that's what these hawks possess who plot their glides
along axes at angles to first rays
triangulating water.
                                        Dawn's pink blaze
resolves into a shimmer of fine lines,
proofs for theorems all;
                                             yet from this lightstrewn path
the hawk's the master lecturer, although
the sun has much to say.
                                             How intricate,
hawk theorems for ellipses, scythe-eyed soar
a geometric text.
                                    He wishes for
the ingenuity that wings bestow
upon these wind glossed patterns;
                                                         imitates
parabolas with mind alone:
                                                  his trace
of lofty genius clouds will soon erase.

HUMILITY

Ingenious, how this stream has sculpted gleam
from sun and rock;
these shallows coalesce
in brilliance that proclaims the sweeping love
of light for smallest atoms, current's swirl
and stone it polishes.
The ceaseless whirl
of water mirrors
circling hawk above
and gnats that spin nearby in sunlight's slash,

Pi's radiance, shell's whorl and midday moon
whose ghostly shimmer
rounds
the eastern sky,
its orbit lecturing astronomy
to clouds and breeze.

He knows his theorems mere
interpretations of much greater minds;

but how he summons pride in his insights,
as water beams, and shimmies with sunlight.

MYSTERY

These shadows spell a word, while roses dance
around late sunlight's edges in the merge
of day and dusk, before the night's black surge
brings on moon's scimitar, starlight's white trance.
He wonders if the word's been spelled by chance,
if roses' revelry emerges from
the chaos of a void, if death's black fruit
is all that will reward his long pursuit
of sensate harmony, math-ordered form,
if nothingness now looms, the last theorem.
"Aglow" is softly blurred by slow twilight,
as chilly breezes hint eternity;
but roses still excite and soothe his sight,
as evening conjures scarlet mysteries.

A RUMOR AT THE ACADEMY

So many years ago, he walked this path.
Familiar—yes—like a recurring dream.
But summer lushness, peace like love that lasts,
sun dappled green are different than they seemed.
For friends have told him matter's mostly space—
atomic structures falsifying spheres,
and painting vacuums senses cannot trace—
all solid is phantasmic. Yes, he fears
this world of desolation, and needs faith,
while all he has is numbers and their truth.
Mortality's gray scythe will never wait
for him to learn how shape and song are rules
of atoms humming now in a faint breeze.

Yet loving seems the light, the weave of leaves.

4.

THE LONELINESS OF EXILE

POWER BEHIND THE THRONE

Emancipator of women, and slaves,
he treats all animals with dignity;
wins influence through his intellect's great fame;
guides Magna Graecia long, benevolently.

This prince though grows reluctant, falls in love
with sunlight's shimmer, pond's geometry,
the formulae for trapezoids oaks weave
in water with their branches' shadows;
he
longs for a life of contemplation of
ellipses hawks inscribe on pale blue sky,
parabolas that swallows swoop.
Insight
means more than all a ruler's riches; light
knows more than scholars at Academy,
and beckons him, a colleague, to be free.

WARNING

The supple gleaming presence of this snake,
her midnight-colored, glistening thin coil,
observed this morning near the sun glazed lake,
unnerves Pythagoras; his daily toil
of studying birds' winged geometries,
the way they intersect with wind and light—
originating angles with the trees—
is halted by this primitive black sight.
But intellect soon subjugates his fear;
he pauses, patient, hoping for a move
expressing undulation. Now a pair
of hungry hawks is circling right above;
he warns the hunted snake, and off she goes;

good use for language learned from cawing crows.

SAVED BY A HAWK

The way the moonlight lathers ancient skin,
the lily-sleek green surface of this pond,
suggests an innocence where light begins,
some perfect purity. His heart responds,
as if its rhythm pulses with the moon,
the incandescent early fireflies,
the sudden verve of spring, green gone too soon.
Just then a sudden chill arrives, denies
the pastoral virginity of May.
He senses stealth and menace in the grove,
as if he's watched on his meek thoughtful way.
The knife of an assassin gleams. Above
a hawk he has befriended starts its dive.
An awesome swoop; blood spurts; and he survives.

THE HOUR OF EXILE

"We want to kill the vegetarian
for all the suffering he's brought on us!"

The arc a torch inscribes on violet sky
suggests a theorem to Pythagoras,
in which flames, multiplied by treachery,
are equal to his doom.
                                        Justice demands
debate with his accusers, but there's no
discussion with a mob, and he must flee—
his family entrusted to his guards—
to safety further north in Italy,

where flames belong to sun and sun alone,
and ethics aren't judged by murderers.

His flight, though bitter, has the rose stealth of
the suddenness of dawn, that hour he loves.

REASSURED BY A HAWK

Vicissitudes of cloud have broken rain
and lightning over every inch of path;

though now the slosh of puddle faintly gleams
in sunsplit respite and placid silence soothes
some spare survivors, (thunder-flattened leaves
still gasping for green air off slashed branches),

sundered trunks of oaks

are everywhere.

                                        He looks, but can't believe

the victory of sever in these woods,

presided over now by vacant sky
and muted trill of lark. Such rule by chance-
sent fury frightens;
                                    theorems disappear
to chaos in a world of garbled ruins.

He's frantic for some order;

                                            hawk ascends,
then traces perfect circles based on Pi.

THE LONELINESS OF EXILE

The sky and water have a love affair
at dawn, covertly, so these woods won't know;
this pond's their rendezvous, its bright skin where
first light's caresses warm and tease, just so,
then heat chill depths into a blaze of lust,
a consummation shimmering, so bright
Pythagoras now shields his eyes. He must
accept that Eros favors even light,
over his logical and abstract soul.

He's like deep woods, secluded; envious,
without a lover who can make him whole.
A cloud concludes pond passion; spent and dark,
the water sleeps again; now he'll discuss
the math of music with a noisy lark.

GOING TO WORK

Triangulate the sun's ascent. Two oaks
the baseline on this steel-chill winter's day.
Diversion, suddenly now, in the way
a hawk bisects bland hemisphere of sky
as if she lectures on geometry
to clouds that hover close. The more he looks
the more he calculates a feathered Pi
that multiplied by gold reveals the light
the hawk explains in her breeze-scything flight
to audience of fluff and haze. But soon,
no warning, hawk dives for its prey below,
a transitory scholar only; now
a blur of angling talons, wings; that's how
the mind is ruled by blood. The dawn's lesson.

THE OTHER

His double sits across the pond marking
the angles of the rising sun and how
they measure water—on an abacus—

just like his own impulse right after dawn
to comprehend anew the calculus
by which light spawns geometry. But who
on earth is this intent Pythagoras—
more youthful, maybe, brown eyes more forlorn—
but otherwise his exact image, now
as sudden breeze melts bronze on water's glass?

Two geese take flight; those fingers count their wings,
one bead per beat, dart quick. He will not ask
and interrupt such rapid figuring,
sleight-of-digits his hand's mirroring.

THE CONCERT

He drinks deep green-veined air
the sun anoints with light;
beholds the way a pair
of thrushes now alight
upon a nearby tree,
and serenade the breeze
with notes in key of "C";

their harmonies amaze,
reveal the depth of art
concealed within this wood;

some mockingbirds now start
a second melody,
such music in their blood
as plays a symphony.

COUNTING TOWARD THE END

A flood of sunlight drenches this lush lawn,
and splashes radiance on nearby trees;
Pythagoras divides the summer dawn
into the cosmos, multiplies by breeze
and quality of drifting yellow light
to calculate how many roses thrive
within the boundary of his circling sight.
His answer's seven but he sees just one,
its scarlet shimmering in early sun.
But faith in truth of math endures despite
this failure; now, as mockingbirds arrive,
their music theorem for math's harmonies,
he calculates how long he might survive
to stroll at dawn, to count the shining leaves.

THE CLOAK

The way late sunshine glances off these stones,
caressing granite with its western light,
and whispering affection to earth's bones
with radiant bronze lust that would invite
hot rapture in the living, soothes him now,
as if he'll be beloved even when
his flesh declines to dust, as if somehow
the sun can feel a passion for old men
through all the darkness of eternity.
And when an eastern breeze begins to tease
mortality from twilight's still warm air,
the chill of exile, loss winged from the sea
on cold foam wings...he fights off his despair,
his shelter the soft cloak that last light weaves.

BEYOND THE CITY

Out here where sunlight lingers in the soil
and hawks display a winged geometry
of loop, ellipse and glide across vast sky
that educates the clouds in how to move,
he feels his aging molecules slow down,
approaching final merge with earth and light
and yet he craves, as when an earnest youth,
this flux of fleeting shapes, revealing truths
of motion, angle, and of grand design.

He lies down in a field so rich with sun
it feels like woven gold, to reconcile
his weariness, with lust to see and prove
the rules of sun etched soar. Lust feels so right,
the only cure for age he'll ever find.

BURIAL OF THE SUN

What hieroglyphs trees' leafy shadows form,
upon a meadow glassbright with the gold
demands of sinking sun upon the warm
blue remnants of a summer day grown old.

Pythagoras can calculate how long
before the sun inters itself once more.
The angled math of shadow's never wrong,
and neither is hypotenuse of soar,

triangulation by ascending hawk,
whose broadwinged glide appears to climb the light.
But how to measure, on his evening walk,
the loss of his brief days to endless night.

A final gleam of bronze enshrines this day.
He ponders brevity. Goes on his way.

THE RIVER

The way the river polishes these stones,
so round and smooth, to perfect little spheres,
reminds Pythagoras of wind on bone,
and how mortality draws ever near.

And yet, how reassuring is the sun,
whose midday flash of gold turns stones to jewels...
He feels revived, as if life's just begun;
however frail the flesh, the mind still rules.

So here begins his love affair with light,
this sleepy afternoon, while river flows.
He lies with her until approach of night;

her kisses warm green water as it goes
on to its rendezvous with shimmering sea.

And ready him for death, if death must be.

5.

MARRIAGE VOWS

MARRIAGE VOWS

Light latticed in the cloud split late day wind,
these gliding geese betray monogamy:
their flock has married Triangle, but now
flirtations with Parabola begin,
a wavering slight infidelity.
A few more scarlet gusts and wing tips show
how curves, ellipses vanish readily
into chaotic fluttering. Allow
for newlywed jitters; it's still a shame
how vagaries of weather overrule
imperatives of form learned in sky school
and consecrated in fresh airborne vows.

Pythagoras, for one, values his name:
he's faithful always to what math proclaims.

A LETTER

Sharp sunlight slashes winter's glaze to bits,
this summer day called February first;
he wastes no wonder on this heat; it fits
his manic mood; his heart's about to burst

with just that sort of joy that doesn't end
so easily, or ever. Lasts as long
as mathematics that the gods intend
as government of harmony, light's song.

Elena's note from Sicily conveys
the news that she's returning in the spring.
No need for algebra; winter's June haze
denotes a sign that makes the noon light sing.

For all the agony, the past's dark glass
is shimmered toward perfection. Love can last!

RETURN

Although the circle is a perfect shape,
it can't compare to his old lover's smile.
This autumn day, they've walked for miles and miles
and all the way, he's craved her crescent lips.

The lake reflects the hour, shadows draped
across its dark blue oval from the pines
that spear the scarlet dusk, and so remind
Pythagoras of how time wars on love.

As if the sky bleeds for their long lost vows.

And yet, they're here; they pause, so motionless
they hear the echo of each other's hearts.
Their kiss is sudden fire; her caress
inspires hope that— now— they'll never part.

No greater hope does earthly life allow.

EPILOGUE: PACIFIST

Pythagoras remembers how he was
the warrior, Euphorbus, slain at Troy;
his bitterness, defeated, in the dust:
his darkly blooming blood, armor destroyed.

His foe Atreides so merciless
in Trojan pride, face venomous and sour
with battle lust, inflicting his torment,
devoid of mercy in the final hour.

But now his world is green, soft breezes lush:
he's been a tree almost two hundred years.
Those fiendish memories drift into mist;
his only enemy is lightning here.

And sometimes he will dream, in still twilight,
of warriors embracing. Soothing sight.